Edge of Southern Bright

Also by Paul Williamson

The DNA Bookshelf
Moments from Red Hill
To the Spice Islands

Paul Williamson

Edge of Southern Bright

Acknowledgements

Poems in this volume have been published in *Quadrant, Short and Twisted; Tamba, Guide to Sydney Rivers; Polestar, Flood, Fire and Famine; Spirit of the Collection; To End All Wars; Positive Words* and *Melaleuca*.

Thanks to family and friends for support and the shared experiences from which I drew.

Thanks also to Les Murray for his support of my poetry and his comments, and to Les Wicks for his poetry edit of the manuscript.

Edge of Southern Bright
ISBN 978 1 76041 466 5
Copyright © text Paul Williamson 2017
Cover: Hawkesbury Sandstone, The Rocks, Sydney

First published 2017 by
GINNINDERRA PRESS
PO Box 3461 Port Adelaide 5015 Australia
www.ginninderrapress.com.au

Contents

Somehow Enduring	9
Near the Edge	11
Reject Depot	12
Risky Business	15
Mining the Past	16
Beneath the Mountain Ash	17
Different Eyes	18
Iron Family	19
Rabbit Casserole	20
Battle Damage	21
World War Monument	22
Booming	23
Christmas dinner at Nana's was crowded	24
Summer Sweat	25
Down the Line	26
For a Crust	27
Sorry Day	28
Resetting Spring	29
The Glinting Road	30
Stairway	31
Brick Canyons	33
Sandstone Stories	35
Home City Visit	36
The Café in the Bookstore	38
Queen Victoria Building	39
Train Space	40
Leaves and Stone	41
The Nicholi Brothers	42
Inner City Hotel	43

In the Library	44
Sheep Paddock	45
Forest for all Seasons	46
Exploring Stories	47
Straight Street	48
Blocking Reality	49
Season Start at Frankston Beach	50
Early Logging Line	51
Almost Silence	52
Midweek Mall	53
Along the Road	**55**
Early Bright	57
River Flowing	58
Roadscapes	60
Slim Town	62
A Rural Town Greens	63
In Season	64
The Start of Days	65
Going Coastal	66
Secluded Hothouse	67
Timber Beams	68
Misty Lane Dairy	69
Boarding School	70
Lake George	71
Suburban Creek Shuffle	72
Around the Docks	73
Puzzles under Water	74
Flying Bridge	75
Dicing for Data	76
Desert Crew	77
Northern Wetlands	78
Detour	79

Fellow Walkers	81
The Weir in the Park	83
Graceful	84
Assyrian Flavours	85
The Next Level	86
On the Outskirts	87
Always Here	88
Degas Riddle	89
Running and Leaping	90
Centenary Anzac Parade	91
Winter Shopping	92
Finding the Calm Place	93
Taking the Break	95
Grand Affections	96
Pushing Back	97
Mixed-up Sunday	98
On the hilltop the slim controller	99
In the Swim Again	100
The Close Distance	101
Occasional Glow	102
Music of Belonging	103
Day Worker	104
Closing the Circle	105

Somehow Enduring

Near the Edge

Above the road is a rusted sheet-iron stable
with a horse outside; an image from past-scattered farms
near where iron-stained clay banks stretched Sydney's water supply
piped from a century ago. Father worked a stint there.

On the downhill side market stalls crowd
the double drive-in theatre normally vacant in daylight.
Antiques are sold, trash and treasure, pets
and greasy food, within surfing music from an ageing band.

Polite people slowly trawl technicolour alleys.
Spanish speaking South Americans offer jewellery;
a too-thin man sells cassettes;
families of heavy islanders scan for bargains;

slender African youths flaunt jaunty masking walks
while an old man and woman show horror-hinting faces;
Muslim fathers herd sons, all in white robes
while up the road the English theme pub draws another crowd.

Reject Depot

'Here was a community of people, hand picked for decades for their 'criminal propensities' and for no other reason, whose offspring turned out to be one of the most law abiding societies in the world.'
– Robert Hughes, *The Fatal Shore*

1.

The Boston Tea Party cancelled voyages
for the criminal poor and rebels of Britain
so the overflow from prison hulks on the Thames
found this southern dumping ground.

The land of eucalypts – new hell, to chop back crime
became for many purgatory;
assigned as unpaid farm labourers
servants, bridge-builders, road-makers.

Pines straight as ships' masts drew
the troublesome to Norfolk Island
after horrors under sail in heaving seas
and the fear of the heavy lash.

Prison there was briefly reforming
but Bloody Bridge captured the road.
Decades later the prison colony closed.
Stone shells of buildings echo the toll.

2.

It was mercy to leave the convict ship
after sailing down the mainland coast
through storms to Van Diemen's Land.

The children were taken to the Orphan Home;
William was ten and Catherine three;
they were not orphans but couldn't stay

with me at the Women's Factory.
We trudged the hill past government buildings
their sandstone rough and hard as our gaolers.

They could call us what they wanted
as we carried our bundles to Molle Street.
The girls could throw it back

as good as it flew.
The guards were criminals
as much as us, mostly needy

who met the hard side of the law.

3.

Others out of prisons
ankles rid at last of chains
were freed in Hobart.

One family trudged the start of winter
along the convict trail to Launceston;
without mother, lost from record;

father with five children, carrying farming tools.
The block was lush but tea tree clawed
as they cleared for farming. Their lives built bleakly.

4.

Founding blood and brutality remain
a backdrop, brash with suspicious whispers.
Some rose to power beneath the stare
of those who thought themselves better.

Now the light of genealogy shows chains
dangling from family trees so the slur fades.
Leaders and bosses still know
they don't own their people's trust.

Risky Business

Westerly gusts herd trees into huddles
chilled beneath a sunless rug of sky.
Eucalypts bend with haunched shoulders
pointing straggled crowns downwind;
lone pines are sharply clipped, aligned.
The sighing static of the low surf reminds
that before guiding satellites
vapour-trailed jets and shopping centres

clippers sped merchants and chancers past the Horn
southeast through the Roaring Forties
to thread the needle between Otway and Wickham Capes.
Some were lost on this Shipwreck Coast like the *Loch Ard*

crashing masts; only two staggering ashore.
On a grassy hill above I manoeuvre on foot and find
the line that sets the near lighthouse above the far
see the killing rocks below and trace

the steady low light, high light course to harbour.

Mining the Past

We drive past prizes along this road
won in the mid-1800s from gold finds
first in the fever fields in Victoria and New South Wales
then across the country.

Miners' tents and wooden shacks sprouted
before solid buildings, paid for through rowdy decades
from rashes of pits sweated into alluvium and mines
that burrowed through blood-spattered rock.

The deluge of European, American and Chinese hopefuls
that unloaded trunks, swags and mining tools
surged on with immigrants and convicts
to reach a surprise quorum for a nation.

Beneath the Mountain Ash

The winding track is lightly muddy
this soggy Belgrave spring. Scrub
to the side is dense and unyielding.
Eucalypts rear their shaggy, honey trunks
to stretch above and straggle. A crimson
rosella darts nervously from a hollow;
there is almost no birdsong
now the nests are charged with eggs.

On the dam below, pacific black and wood ducks
cruise with moorhens beneath a shore
lined by giant columns of mountain ash
that rear like images from past millennia.
Along the valley floor a muddy creek
snakes past snags and undercut banks.
On its sides yellow flowers stare from ground cover
at the 200-metre line of pale, pure lilies
that stutter to the dam then scatter behind the bulrushes
as if dabs of a colonial sense of beauty.

Different Eyes

When a lost child stopped in local legend
shadows wandered beneath straggled branches
of wattle, tea tree and eucalypt, bright
light shone off gum leaves and sunburnt grass.

Forests on their artist canvases stopped straining
to be European countryside
a hundred years after the first fleet.
Tom Roberts lead the group on the steam train

for Box Hill Station then Houston's farm
to camp the nights and follow a French way;
painting in open air with Heidelberg impressionist
friends, Conder, Abrahams, McCubbin

Brooke Hansen, Jane Sutherland and Streeton.
Near Blackburn Lake they captured orchards, bushscapes
morning and evening glow, butterflies and blossoms
a bush burial and southern idyll.

Iron Family

On the early eastern growth corridor
between the city and logging in the ranges
Bayswater Park boasts a sandstone bubbler base
with a brass plaque to the crowning of a young queen.
Nearby a metal goanna lies on a rock
and concrete hippopotamuses swim
in a pool of ground-down rubber tyres
while children play in a wood and rope jungle-gym.

Slender eucalypts stretch above
the corrugated iron shelter
that shades the retired steam engine
now a sturdy climbing frame
chipped and painted black and red
to shining protection. Instrument gaps are sealed
with metal covers. Round-capped rivets
grip the lesser joins. Heavy bolts bond plates.

I knock my knuckle on the coal tender
and sense the solid wall. I have not met
you before but I have travelled with your cousins
the iron ships, around our coasts and to the pack ice.
There is a family resemblance.

Rabbit Casserole

Nana made tasty rabbit casseroles.
The depression had honed her skills.
Grandfather caught the rabbits
during nights as a factory security guard

after he lost his job as storeman.
His traps were set near the Parramatta River
where warrens spread beneath the grass
but the family struggled to survive.

The army at least paid a wage and his going
might save his sons enlisting; they did.
He died at Tobruk.

Battle Damage

The drunk gave the curly-haired infant a silver coin
as he sat well-behaved between parents
on the park bench. They were tolerant,
respectful, even if slightly worried.

It was the child he could not have
with what the war had left of him;
or if he had a child like the veteran father
the one he could not live with.

The football field was unarmed combat.
Two ex-soldiers finished the playing life
of an opponent in seconds.
After the game they had a drink.

It was a fairly normal battle.

World War Monument

Down the hill the Repatriation Hospital
helped victims of mustard gas
from the war a generation before
live out lives in treatment.

Looming below cream funnels
the multi-storey towers of buff bricks
had regretful semi-permanence as wards
of gas patients slowly emptied.

Booming

Smokes and drinks needed money;
too much money for father to spend
when children slept four to a room in bunks.

Christmas presents were shoes or coats on layby
grown into by winter in five months' time;
if there were no hand-me-downs.

They didn't feel poor;
the family down the tree-lined road
had a dirt floor in their kitchen.

Boys and girls ironed clothes, some cooked;
older ones carried around the younger
feeding bottles and changing towelling nappies.

Kids swarmed for cricket in the backyard
for rounders out the front.
Billy carts rattled the road.

The family van was mass transport
for family visits, church and shops.
It bulged with holiday luggage.

Bullying was forbidden to avoid chaos;
fights were verbal and mostly ignored;
minds academic like their parents

through years of Commonwealth scholarships;
terror for girlfriends at the Sunday table.
In that fibro world truth was spoken and agreed.

Christmas dinner at Nana's was crowded

indoors, almost protected from the Sydney summer
by double brick and a between-wars veranda.
She served turkey with vegetables and ham
then hot plum pudding with threepences and custard.
It must have brought back memories of her English husband
who could have grown up with that Christmas.

He left his name in the war memorial
written on the wall where red poppies grow.
His name was Edwin; my middle name an homage.
His body never came home
so Nana may have hoped
he would somehow find his way back alive
to breed his canaries in the backyard cage.

Christmas lunch this year is umbrella-shaded;
seafood and salad, my family sitting festive
around the sturdy garden table.

Summer Sweat

People not held at daily grind
shelter indoors or head for pools;
infants are put into showers and baths.
Rail lines buckle so trains are cancelled.

In the western suburbs night heat is brutal
within still air that ends summer;
children awake and sweating in bed
on sheets and mattresses, far

from any breath of sea breeze
without fans or air conditioning.
The heat is heavy
not the thin searing blast

at Christmas lunch
when it seems to fade after dark.
The question nags. Will it cool
enough for a sheet as cover?

Down the Line

When rescue meant belt and line
father's body trundled
ramrod straight ahead of foaming white
that edged the turquoise.

At eight I learned the ocean buoyed
so sunny swimming started
with five metre sprints
catching rides on small breaks.

Christmas tides roared the best surf
high hills with rumbling white scree
rides with speed bumps over backwash;
even riding lesser dumpers

with torso half out front
above churning sand;
now my son rides those slopes
down a curling line.

For a Crust

Beneath the trailing branch
of dull cream eucalypt blossoms
that sweep the head of the tall priest
who intones the ritual prayers, the lilting
fiddle sings rose petals into the grave.

The deceased has a name from Donegal
via Narrabri eighty years before
then Sydney for Christian Brothers school
marriage and a job in the Public Service
interrupted by air force duty.

Government work was his father's too;
he had been a station master
the son, a state administrator;
careers that stayed possible
amid the fear from beating rusted shields.

Sorry Day

Today the rain is tears.
Before the flow was often blood
poured out through centuries.

On this day of apology
drops fall on breaking smiles.
Respect is shown

for the journeys of First Peoples;
turning to what should lie ahead.

Resetting Spring

Seasons are clerically decreed
from the Antarctic to the high tropics
as the earth is squeezed into four sizes.

Here blossoms blast in midwinter;
kookaburras cackle territory;
a galah gnaws the mouth of last year's nest hollow.

First People quietly ignore the folly
and keep on calling the many more seasons
when and how they come.

The Glinting Road

Blocks of villas sprout relentlessly between houses
as we drive towards car and tram crowded Sydney Road.
Mature grape vines and olive trees of migrant families
from hungry times in Sicily and the Boot
grow next door to reaching cottage gardens of Ten-pound Poms.
Further along the red-brick church has a Vietnamese Mass.
The street is hemmed with dense melaleucas
until a spreading eucalypt centres the roundabout.

The taxi driver grew up near the Road
with fewer restaurants and no night life;
he had to go to the city to drink.
He thinks it better now though it killed
an Irish woman in a night alley. Bars
and supermarkets sit beside bridal and bargain shops.
A Turkish gift store sparkles across from fish and chips.

We eat cheese triangles with falafels in a Lebanese bakery
drink coffee, smiling under statues of a mullah and the Virgin;
while painful need and want search out Eden.

Stairway

Events trouble and surprise
but quickly become the norm
a base camp for the next trail
climbed sometimes wearily

up slopes where each step
becomes a ledge to perch
before the clouded path beyond;
a track strained with twists

that obscure ascended heights
until a chance look back
reveals that life
took a different turn

from where we thought
we would see our future.

Brick Canyons

Sandstone Stories

Wind and water carve streaked galleries
into sandstone behind wave shaped beaches.
Clans painted dreamtime images
on the buff-orange walls of the caves.

Convicts chiselled slabs that say Sydney;
different blocks that quarries gave up
were purgatory or easy paradise
carted for buildings and bridges.

Father showed the children, time's pictures
on sheer rock faces; pebble bands and
sediment beds sweeping and flattening
as honey ribbons and weathered chocolate breaks.

Near family picnics in Stanwell Park
trees clung to bluff tops, anchoring
into joints between the massive rock cubes.
Sandstone and eucalypts left roots in our minds.

Today we walk a path through The Rocks
and see the marks from convict picks
on the sheer face behind a stone-won warehouse
glimpsing the stories in earth's canvas.

Home City Visit

Old buildings sport proud monograms
founding dates and claims of purpose;
Hawkesbury sandstone faces on bottom floors.
Higher walls are rendered and painted, or red brick
and stone retell stories obscured
by facades on futuristic high rise temples to commerce.

Close to our hotel at the edge of Chinatown.
shop fronts flash neon lights touting
small endeavours. I jaywalk the busy street
dodging traffic as ever, comfortable and anonymous.
There is love on these streets, families and friends.
Ahead two homeless men chat on the footpath;

their beards are long and their clothes grubby
as they stroll, enveloped by the purpose driven crowd.
Others travel hard behind faces marked by addiction.
On the lawn an ibis feeds, plastic tagged to track its vagrancy.
Art in the park shows Sydney's beaches, fishing, toil and entitlement
that can't be seen from fibro houses on the outskirts.

A statue of Captain Cook claims he discovered this country.
The war memorial stands in the style of the Britain
Australia fought for and paid out blood; Grecian soldiers
slay a minotaur in the fountain.
At the Domain speakers proclaim.
Two police at the edge of the crowd

show mild interest while they chat
on closely clipped grass; edges cut sharp.
People stroll within the clatter of a leaf blower
and the muffled din of city traffic. Workers trudge
to nearby commerce earnestly talking their business
while young lovers lie close and kiss on the lawn.

A homeless man wanders past a gnarled old
eucalypt towards his swag beneath a Moreton Bay fig.
Down the grassy hill shines Sydney Harbour where First People
gathered shellfish before the sandstone soils
and hard times greeted colonists. In a multicoloured
carpet of small craft, tall ships celebrated the bicentennial.

The sandstone cathedral nearby rears as a rigid twist
to the code of love. Inside a Filipino woman kneels and prays
as Saint Patrick guards the door. The local saint that Irish bishops
thought the troublesome colonial woman, is outside in brass
where jacarandas blaze their lavender statement.

The Café in the Bookstore

This large old Sydney store is relentlessly
colourful and eye catching to bring in sales.
I sit watching, preoccupied
as authors blink in and out of mind
while my eyes scan shelves and subjects.

Videos claim a corner; board games own some shelves;
cooking utensils hang unexpectedly
for those inspired by the cookery books.
The café where we eat all-day breakfast
serves chef-style salmon and poached eggs.

The books I came for are on dangerous
reptiles and amphibians for my grandson
and a Latin dictionary for me.
Poets feature sparsely;
one crafted line for two thousand words of prose.

My life seems mostly guided by single lines.

Queen Victoria Building

Next to the town hall but looking more fun
is the Romanesque gift of a Sydney recession;
with its rounded columns and broad arches
balustrades, floors tiled in Mediterranean colour;
patterns diverging and converging like a walking conversation
and a leaf and vine motif on iron latticework.

Cafés in the arcade are crowded
to end the business lunch hour; office workers
talk and eat, discuss their trades; a young woman
smiles and chats with her male friend. Patrons
in the stack of shops seem mostly European
or Asian tourists. Service energy is intense

in this concert hall turned mall;
a monument that basks refurbished
after surviving cycles of threats.

Train Space

This afternoon there is a wedding reception;
last week a Chinese art installation.
The giant shell shows the marks of work and rest
on walls scrubbed towards clean
where dull green over duller white paint
at times layered with decades of dust
is trimmed with grease ghosts from heavy equipment.

Electrical control boxes protrude, unconnected;
ends of water pipes and wooden pegs are cropped flush.
Repairs to stonework are cunningly blended
brick or Hawkesbury sandstone
around windows where gothic iron arches
cup panes of ancient frosted glass
that helped light the sweat of Carriageworks.

An unused heavy crane boasts
a lift of ten tons to build and repair carriages
near where the cellar door is bolted and sealed; part of the finish
of a café where floors of aggregate concrete
with embedded rails are ground flat and polished
where people come for echoes of the age of steam.

Leaves and Stone

Sunny sandstone guards the stories
of healthy confinement;
different realities and eyes
that saw them and lived them;
movement only some saw
voices only some heard.

Students amble in the leafy grounds
study, and chat in historic halls
trying to prepare
for the shifting world outside.

The Nicholi Brothers

(eucalyptus nicholi)

Traffic fumes, down the blaring road
wall in urban music in the coffee shop.
Factories crowd warehouses
feeding the city food distributors
and nearby shopping centres.

Across the road the brothers flourish.
They have risen in the crush
opportunists, located between a high
brick wall, electric and phone wires
and melaleucas at either side.

Their life is good, with carbon dioxide
from trucks and water from coastal rain.
They stretch above the urban grime
to own a sun in city haze.

Inner City Hotel

The plastic, soulless nook
looks crisp and modern
designed for fleeting stays

by tired businessmen or
parties without troubling fixtures.
Parking a car in the cramped space

is like passing a driving test.
At the front desk the clerk stops married couples
from moving independently.

Repeat custom is unlikely
so cut price offers blare.
It is a place to sleep. Thank you.

In the Library

In the national temple
to the written word

books and computers shine
with science, politics, diverse arts

history and environment
to teach and entertain

slant to match the authors' minds;
perhaps inspire their readers.

This talk is froth on the deep reserve of words.

Sheep Paddock

Partial truth flies in flurries
where early sheep had grazed
below this hill with trees mauled down
by spreading colonists
and planted back to flower crimson.

Black Mountain Tower pierces low haze;
wattles shine golden by the winding road.
Workers surprise their ministers
with sound advice from planning offices
on flat ground in the bush capital

to help miss recession leaving a rare world
enclave for lives less troubled.

Forest for all Seasons

The kiosk at the zoo for trees
is fashioned for the tourist trade
with an airy playground and restaurant.

The needle tower hovers above.
Eucalypts loiter sparsely on surrounding hills
below the brooding Brindabellas.

The view across to parliament, over shining
Lake Burley Griffin and garden suburbs
is still verdant in this late summer.

At the Arboretum most plants are young.
On a hill stands the wide brown monument
to the earth worm, a hero of the project.

Nearby old cedars grow darkly, straight and intriguing
around a tasteful toilet and picnic tables.
Cyclists grunt towards the scrap iron eagle's nest.

Joggers shuffle thinly along the road.
An exhibit shows plants that can stand
the Canberra chill and heat.

Exploring Stories

Grey stone and mock Tudor entwined
under his skills as artist/architect
to birth this sprawl of eclectic buildings.
Son of a Norwegian master mariner
Justus Jorgensen dreamed up this artists' complex;
formed it from pressed earth, stone and brick.

Sculptors, printmakers and artists
worked and lived here except during war
when the grounds were market gardens.
Now lawns are graced by statues
while in the rooms hang paintings on canvas
linen, wood, linocuts, etchings and prints.

Montsalvat subsists with national money;
not the directed passion of a visionary
or the focused core of an expressive school
but a blood line still exploring.

Straight Street

Near the law courts, the coffee shop is claimed by art;
framed crowds of long faces in sombre colour.
Outside a barrister in a curled wig hurries past
flowing black tails. A solicitor lugs
an armful of briefs, tows a wheeled case.

A white-collared advocate scuttles with her harried clerk.
while more legal workers walk straight and tall;
so much black and white. Students evolve
towards the same posture, with stumbles of gravitas
over texting. Pedestrians pass unfocused;

some perhaps, the fodder of the legal grind. Rebellious
street trees stretch up towards sky
between tall buildings. Up the hill on Williams Street
hi-vis jackets brighten workers in a park.

Blocking Reality

Cigarette smoke is thick as sacrifice to the instant.
Festive balloons are caught in trees by strings.
Stilt-walking spruikers in buffed costumes
throw caps and T-shirts to the baying crowd.

Nearby the closed queue has smiles dancing on their faces
excited to see a match to real faces
from their TV sets at home. I sense the thrill
like a phone ringing in someone else's room.

Clothes are crisp from budget stores.
Near the entry door devotees wait with thin lines for mouths
on strained faces. A surge of envy erupts as a group finishes
and leaves. A woman scurries away in triumph with her souvenirs.

Sponsors' tents fill the adjoining block of land, their banners
shout overhead to the drone with the camera.

Season Start at Frankston Beach

Heavy wind and blowing rain have cleared
along the stretched edge of the bay
where immature seagulls squawk to be fed
by their adults squabbling for scraps.
In the hard scrub birds nearby hop distractedly
to glean food after the cold.

The ocean is waveless. On the shallow shelf
sand bars trap small ponds to gleam at the shore
near the long, salt bleached jetty.
The shack store where we buy coffee
opened yesterday for the new season.
Today bathers return with sun-shunned bodies

to wade along the water's edge. A toddler
determinedly trails his grandfather. Children
work imaginations on drift wood, shells and a puffer fish
left to die by an early morning angler.
Older families migrate slowly along the foam line
while young lovers sit close in shallows and kiss.

Fashions surprise, building collages, contrasting
colours and patterns against a grey standard and hair tints
meant to be worn with evening frocks. Dogs wander
with little fuss as unready skins turn distressed red
striped by lines from shoulder straps.

Early Logging Line

Volunteers hold steam engines to shining laurel and brass
as smiling tourists climb aboard open carriages
for the Puffing Billy line in the Dandenongs.

On a siding behind its bars and lock
a metal mail carriage surrenders to rust.
Nearby a dull white explosives van corrodes.

Between the two rusty carriages a juvenile
mountain ash is framed, telegraph-pole straight
with cinnamon ribbons and a single knot of ochre staining.

Near the station, ground was cleared to store the logs
that early timber workers cut and hauled
to trains for wood to help build Melbourne.

Now in the yard, trees reach out of the earth
stretching strongly for the sun
as the forest makes its claim.

Almost Silence

Our search of Hobart's bookstores is fruitless
but convict days must have left voices.
Old tomes that yellow on the shelves

tell of Truganini, and Hell's Gate
as entrance to wilderness
forgetting the reasons for its name;

prison torment edging roaring ocean
at a freezing western logging port.
Gaol cells at Port Arthur and stone bridges

draw tourist cameras and buses.
The shadows there are not questioned
to make some sense of the murmurs

that groan in brains of descendants.
At last we find the lingering illness explained
by a visiting poet who surgically reveals

the disdain that preserves the infirmity.

Midweek Mall

People with varied skin hues and ages amble
in diverse clothes, striped, check, plain or patterned;
some in black wearing the veil.
A workman in khaki shorts and heavy
boots, hurries by on smoko.
Tight black cotton almost covers the couple
gym-buffed, lips curled, who berate a tracksuited woman.

Nearby tasks twitch on a thin computer
while a student accepts noodles from mother who works
behind the burger joint's island counter.
A toddler pushes a stroller while his older brother rides.
A man with Tourette's shouts an outburst
as he shuffles DVDs outside a store
in the open area that dilutes tension.

A woman, frail and grey, shopping trolley as walking aid
helps a man who wears the pallid mask of vascular stress.
Well-worn men with Mediterranean looks
retain their table to talk over coffee.
Outside a rust-trimmed car rumbles
and the complimentary bus waits.

Along the Road

Early Bright

A glowing horizon calls
from beyond the mustard fields
and woolly-blanket forests

beneath a sky washed to pastel
and budding straight-based clouds
that trail errant wisps.

The morning light
paints rocks rust and mauve
polishes leaves on gums

lightens shadows
sparkles the windy lake
clears the road into the distance.

River Flowing

We catch the flat recent ferry past the rescued shore
lined by reaching mangroves with laurel leaves.
Bulbuls reap the olive-coloured fruit from higher branches;
cormorants scan from vantage points above open water.

Factories hide behind foliage and are barely seen;
stone or large bricks as mimics, line the banks;
heaps of broken industrial pipes are drafted;
concrete slabs and pylons hold back highest walls.

We don't see floating rubbish, just rare dead sticks.
as the ferry glides commuters to Sydney Harbour
along channels dredged for navigation lanes
guarded by rounded red and green posts.

Parramatta where eels swim, in First People's tongue
was an inland port for early hard settlement.
Grazing and farming land saw convicts graft
the town and bridges from Hawkesbury sandstone

then carve graffiti into least obvious stone.
Later the female orphanage was set by the river
inside a looming government complex;
an asylum seen from the road when I was young

when the river was a watery rubbish tip.
Industries spewed chemical garbage
joining household refuse, fridge shells and building waste.
The mangrove swamps were poisonous ooze.

Fish were there but too toxic to eat.
Bull sharks still visited; hopeful bathers found
one in the wooden baths near Ryde Bridge.
But now the noxious smell has left my childhood river.

The mottled brick once asylum, pressure cleaned
is on a university campus close to calm water.
The river, no longer a ragged flow out of urban outskirts
is protected, clasped to a city's breast.

Roadscapes

1.

The fork in the concrete road calls us south
to Gundagai away from closest Yass;
fast driving either way. Bottlebrush
flowerless but dense from enough rain

hems the way past rural history;
poplars and old conifers near farm buildings
a red apple tree, loaded on the divide
between this road and the way back.

In the paddocks dead tree sculptures
rise above scrub like bleached vanities;
broken forms in different shapes.
Fatal shrines warn passing drivers.

2.

A tree-flecked hill glows like a mustard sun.
Hard-grazed grass shows dust patches
down to the long straw of the verge
as the journey twists to default.

Further along golden brown tufts shine like lamps
above stubble cropped by buff-coloured cattle
that straggle down the slope in morning sunlight
towards standing straw near the road.

3.

In the next paddock the time-smoothed hills
are bare and dotted with dusty mounds;
at first glance, tussocks some with radiating grass crowns

but then surprise heads show and loose skin
on hungry sheep between thirsty clumps.
Under duress both look alike.

In nearby vineyards the bore water saved
crop is purple-ripe away from southern fires;
for an escapee vintage.

4.

Leaving the country wedding
we drive through wide rolling hills
heavily grazed by sheep.

Relic grass is low-standing stubble.
Black cattle graze the long paddock
barely holding condition.

Creek banks are dusty dry
and without their turf lining.
A green rug of grass spreads

in the shadow of low mountains.
The clouds have decreed
what will feast and what must struggle.

Slim Town

The town is on a protracted diet.
Near the centre, red-brick buildings hold
their age; the school and houses are trim.
At the pub the barmaid serves where bushrangers
met and planned to rob a coach
of miner's gold but shot a policeman.

On the wall, pictures are of bullock teams
hauling massive logs from eucalypt forests.
Now wood is often plantation pine;
sheep and cattle still graze the mustard hills
but roads have taken the shops to nearby large towns
where many work to live here.

White arms wave from the wind farm, to visitors
and those who leave and sustain.

A Rural Town Greens

The sandstone church with pure, high statue
centres the crisp, clean town
with its rust-coloured bricks and rendered walls.
Tidy parks and gardens speak of work in time to fill.
They help lure the highway tourist trade
through pea-soup-tiled shopfronts
to buy household wares, clothes and antiques.
Decent rain has at last washed walls
and lifted paint in non-obvious places.

Beside the bypassing highway where the bullocky cursed
his treacherous brass dog for fouling the tuckerbox
the wooden skeleton of a bullock wagon stands house solid
with hardwood tray and spokes, iron-rimmed wheels.
Beside it the Limestone Inn fades in ruins;
built from country stone and mortar bulked with stream-bed rubble
it gleaned the passing trade before bushrangers robbed it.

In a nearby yard a Sunshine harvester, workhorse
and former rural hero displays in disrepair
iron cutting combs contorted and rusty.
A companion tractor decays beside it.
The bones of the drivers are in the ground
but their blood flows in arms that tend farms
and sheep and cattle that endured the dry
and graze into condition on the hills.
Shining mechanical farm muscle
revs across the highway from paddock to paddock.
The feel is relief and the hope that rain restocks.

In Season

It seems an insult to nature to abandon
an orchard lush and heavy with fruit

the gift unharvested
the grower unrewarded

the picker unfulfilled
the town people poorer

when buyers look overseas
where labour costs are less.

Plums will not be picked
when the trees are cleared away.

The Start of Days

Our home is on a tree-lined slope;
my wife, out of contact.
She might come. Worried, we wait
before we leave for Nana's.

The phone rings. Bundle children
into the car. Fires burn near the road.
Do you see smoke? Yes.
Do you see flames? No.

Still time to be safe
while crews work through the night
to stop and save.
By dawn the heat and wind are gone.

Cars on the road to home
seem less worried.
Our house still stands
covered in soot and smell of fire.

Smoke ribbons rise from tree stumps.
Time to clean, reclaim our lives
until the next peak fire time.
The start of days.

Going Coastal

The road is carved into embankment;
a forest above and forest below
where falling angels roll.

Lunging speedsters flash lights
behind law abiding dawdlers
who ponder written speed

as vainglorious.
Gum trees with purple high blood
pressure blotches lean to watch.

At last along the coastal highway, salty
weather-blasted trees posture age;
blow-in white trumpet flowers shine.

Shopping centres grow and sport alluring signs.
An apartment compound rears high fences;
heavy metal gates hinting of unseen crime.

New granite spreads the cemetery.
Beach haunts are clean
crowded with moving colours.

My father's holiday cottage
sold when driving got too hard
stands on a street where an ambulance waits.

Secluded Hothouse

The long dirt road quizzes cars
about their off road worthiness
and guards the Bundanon homestead
from undetermined visitors.

Spotted gums and dark shaggy eucalypts
set a frame for dense vines;
rock faces drop to cleared fields
below Pulpit Rock by the Shoalhaven.

The homestead the Boyd family cherished
has solid sandstone houses and timber outbuildings.
A bark canoe rests on a veranda.
Near the house jacaranda snow covers the lawn.

Magnolias flower grandly; branches laced with lichen.
In the paddocks dirt brown cattle graze.
By the small lake rippled with windy waves
rock benches cluster beneath stretching branches.

Perhaps the bush and river still had too much to tell
after Arthur's ten day first visit.
Later he bought this place, and built the warm light studio
of local cedar for family art and sculpture.

Canvases filled from the forest and river;
surged like the river after rains; landscapes
linked to the Divine. Painting like a poet
he unveiled nature's glint, feelings and questions.

Now it belongs to us all. He knew
this haunt with its lessons could have no single owner.

Timber Beams

From within the grass and scrubby trees
at the forest roadside
two white giants taper
smooth round trunks

that stretch to thin crowns reaching
for light from near the edge
of the rain forest gully.
Sparse bark ribbons hang low

to where yellow robins flit.
Side branches send straggling leaves
from the straight, giving hardwood.

Misty Lane Dairy

In drowsy highland predawn
the steaming herd would wait in shifting discomfort at the gate.
They were friesians with some jerseys for higher cream
that wandered in to have udders cleaned, milk started
suction cups fitted, to fill the silver cans for the roadside.

Each cow was named; I knew them all. Ilene could kick
your brains loose, objecting to being cleaned;
Frying Pan could only fit that below her udder
when she was full of milk. The possum
Roger the Lodger lived in the roof;

stretching for bread with cream and strawberry jam.
There was one bull but most semen was bought.
An AI man arrived to artificially impregnate
when the other cows mounted to call time.
Stainless steel chains helped difficult births.

Female calves grew to place in the herd;
vealers were quickly sold or had rubber rings
fitted to die off testicles for steers.
If a dangler escaped so a young bull steamed the paddocks
an antiseptic blade guided by thick fingers
returned the needed order to the cycle.

Boarding School

You smile remembering happy days.
My visit here brings uncertainty
about my skew of memory.

There are vineyards now around this rural school
that helped to shape us.
Classrooms are used by adult study groups;

new buildings claim gaps.
The sports oval sits unused in long grass;
around it dark pines still loom.

Away from loving parents, siblings
assumed rites of passage
we lingered in rural isolation.

Lake George

A boating group drowned
under sudden shallow waves

a generation ago, bringing gales of grief.
Now lush shoots cluster around shrinking puddles

where sheep and cattle graze above water
drawn down by alluvial bores.

Wind farms wave white arms from hills
to the cars on the highway.

The lake waits to rise in the wet.

Suburban Creek Shuffle

The smell of fox shrouds
the dewy morning and the leaf carpeted trail
between giant mountain ash
clothed in leathery ribbons.

A brown tree creeper skitters upward
near a hollow burnt by a long-forgotten fire.
Beneath the high canopy, leaves are spattered
with droppings and downy white feathers.

Down the slope, splashes of feral
orange flowers glow. A duck flaps
as if trying to escape the water that flows
out of houses, beneath the traffic and exhaust

into the rippling creek that feeds the lake
close to this road through the Yarra Ranges.
A sign says platypus live in this water;
they are dated oldest in the country.

On the asphalt path through the park
dogs and their owners take each other for walks
past where council weed cutters growl
at the sign of the Friends of Monbulk Creek

whose next working bee is unscheduled.
A stump is sprouting dogged shoots
where a falling tree broke the bridge rail.
Will the bridge to nature stay in repair?

Around the Docks

Tourists bustle through Salamanca markets;
cafés and fish restaurants crowd the dock
near where ocean racers cross the line.

Iron bollards and wooden beams endure
behind tyres that brace for when ships breast.
When timber splinters they call in concrete.

Ice ships farewell the grey wharf
for heaving seas near Antarctic bases.
The harbour fades into distance.

Convicts landed here near hard government buildings.
Settlers huts were ramshackle wood
beside red-brick warehouses that eked out commerce.

Kangaroo meat saved the colony.

Puzzles under Water

Heavy hardwood planks
line the pier beside the iron ship
its crimson paint chipped and daubed.
Sharp hulls like this are built for icy seas
and crews of Viking blood.

Diesel and salt air perfume
the cabin, work space and low fantail
as the ship's wake churns south.
Scientists trail borrowed, rarely used equipment
to listen to the ocean's story.

Water attacks and garbles readings.
We cut the damaged cable away, remould contacts
for the same frustrating noise.
The cure is tried again and again
with dogged faith in thinking

until stories read for days and weeks
of the ocean's birth, written in sea-floor stone.
Mother Carey's chickens tend their watery barnyards;
the seas are patrolled by wanderers.

Flying Bridge

Watchmen on the bridge
of this horned navy mine sweeper
stand in the breath of sea spray.
Tropical breezes stroke faces
as flying fish flash above danger.

The day glows and seas are slight
as we sail for Lord Howe Island.
Our flying bridge is not heroic
like storm blown watches on Royal Navy ships
that spawned the North Atlantic tradition.

A bulk carrier looms without right of way
or any sign of watchers on their bridge
snug behind a wall of glass.
They don't answer radio calls;
will not divert their path.

Dicing for Data

My shirt is sacrificed
to the drilling rig and its grease
as I cling and climb towards the viewing ledge.
I am using sonic vision on this research rig
air gun pops instead of bat chirps
to see through water and a thousand metres of rock
siting drill holes down-dip of wells where they won't get gas kicks;
a light weight, non-industry system but it works.

From the platform a three quarter tropic ring
of low island might be a West Australian reef.
But this one has killed; it is the ruins of Krakatoa
that built a giant volcano from thick lava
then blocked it to blow its island apart.
The tidal wave found and drowned
thousands without warning in Indonesia.
Its child grows again under worried eyes.

Our varied group does reverse exploring
trying not to find the gas that scares scientists.
Early wells here took kicks that jammed drill stems;
we fools are drilling with no blow-out preventers.
My bombardier's trick of throwing buoys to site holes
works but the chemists' final sample says gas below.
We avoid the shock we can foresee.

Desert Crew

In the land of red dust, sun and saltbush
boots and denim shorts, daily litres of water
we head the land rover and cruiser off-road
scrub bashing towards melanoma
sleeping in tents, eating salad and grilled steaks
surveying minerals lines after the wet.

Kangaroos here are red, emus fast, goats feral
salt lakes, the swimming holes that slowly dry to pans.
Fortnightly weekend home is Coolgardie
where the company house waits for beer and rest. We play
two up among the trees, cars parked like a wrecking yard;
fists of notes as two coins spin to the concrete floor.

A workmate pours beer on his cornflakes, climbs trees
through the night. After he leaves us he kills himself.
The boss gets fired for taking the Land Rover
to Perth to visit his girlfriend.
He still works with us through his notice week;
good of him to do his share.

Northern Wetlands

The land about dozes under a red blanket
as the dry lingers.
We reach the wetlands harbouring life
then boat along the Yellow River
beneath mossy, stretching growth.

Ibis and spoonbill delve on muddy edges.
Ducks feed heads down
tails up in mirky flows.
Kingfishers snatch insects
out of humid, sticky air.

A jacana walks on a lily pad;
like a Jesus bird on water. Crocodiles
and kites seize the weak and unwary
but life expands so strongly
dealers in death cannot stop it.

Detour

Fleeing the traffic jam freeway
with children fussing in the back
our road relives
childhood journeys to grandparents.

A thin tree bends and stretches
from the wall of roadside coastal scrub.
High grass feeds familiar dairies.
Jersey cows watch our progress.

Hairpin bends break the way
through sandstone past a picnic ground
found when young, on foot;
before fast tarmac fires us

wanting another detour.

Fellow Walkers

The Weir in the Park

Cars would drive over the childhood weir
shepherded surely to safety.
It dammed a swimming pool
near picnics under Parramatta trees.
After rain its illegal water ride
surged with bucking rubber tubes.

Father, solid like the old weir
that night all alone, ceased to remember
beneath the steady flow; the family unaware
a lurking fault was widening to fail.
We found him lost in the morning
when crumpling foundations could not hold.
Tears flow, less steady than the river.

Graceful

She repeats the dance
again and again, straining for rhythm
while her little niece watches absorbed.
The steps will flow tomorrow
with a partner on a better floor.

Her martial arts forms
even if slightly businesslike
are a joy to see;
a young girl's crisp movement;
even the head kick.

Assyrian Flavours

A flute and six drummers dance the groom
into the brimming reception;
musicians bright in white gowns
head ties, festive dark beards.

His mother's people are Assyrian Australian
here to celebrate in numbers.
His father's blood is Anglo Irish
a steady family, present in force.

After speeches women circle dance
twirling dancing veils held at each end
joyful arms above their heads
as the music pounds towards frenzy.

The bride's father walked her down the aisle
at the seaside church in Wollongong
looking like he would rather keep than give.
Later a prayer nodded darkly for distant dying relatives.

The Next Level

I have been given a promotion
from Grandad to Grandpa.
The rank is phonetically higher
because of the plosive 'p'.

To grand-infants I was Grandad.
As one grew and watched TV, he asked
with a wistful look, did I shrink
to pocket size to help in anxious moments?

Others watch programs and cartoons
with Grandpa as moderate mastermind.
I hope I am that clever
and can rise to the new rank.

On the Outskirts

In the threading crowd at Tuesday's outdoor market
stocky islanders clad in tracky daks with top-down hoodies
and black-veiled Middle Eastern women
with their short-haired olive-skinned children
mix with parents with blonde curly-haired infants
while older people shop leaning on trolleys.

The crowd isn't from coffee-charged office and factory crews
but people unscheduled by this industrial rim
in the Ranges at a fingertip of Melbourne Metro.
Fruit and fish, meat and vegetables colour stalls;
onions, potatoes and pumpkins are bargains
like the birthday cards, electricals and clothing.
Space is left in car boots for the trip to the cut-price grocer.

Security guards in black and hi-vis yellow watch
those who need low prices for fuller lives.

Always Here

Sidewalk hands are outstretched
beside signs that ask for money
to hold on to troubled life.

But aren't they like you and me?
Can't they care for themselves?
But some are ill or injured

some are single parents;
some need the skills for work;
some cannot learn or plan;

some just follow their parents' road;
so Henry Lawson's struggling
mates support their underdogs.

Degas Riddle

He mostly finds the point of ugliness
in dumpy female nudes, dancers in Paris
with twisted faces; horses and jockeys
at awkward speed; worried family groups;
well dressed people with unselfconscious oddities.

He shows the plain truth not the dream
except perhaps when painting his sister as friend
or a lady artist with paint-stained fingers
as fond companion, or chocolate box
pictures of pink-frilled ballerinas.

Sometimes he paints from duty
like repaying family to earn his stay
in New Orleans. But if beauty can save us
is it the beauty in ordinary people?

Running and Leaping

Adam and Buddy fly with the Swans;
Archie kicked a round ball record;
Kathy was faster than the world's best;
the nation's Rugby League captain is First People.

Their bodies' age old strength
travelling long distance on foot
for hunting, food and ritual
holds an inheritance

of speed and endurance
now to run and compete;
another way to earn a living
win fame and social strength.

Centenary Anzac Parade

On the town's main street light horse ride first;
uniforms dark green not khaki, cartridge belts crossing chests
with a nurse in long dress and red and white cloak.
Grandfather joined from the bush for World War I.
He won a military medal for youthful bravery
keeping communications open.

Banners from conflicts file down High Street:
Boer War, World Wars I and II with Kokoda Section
Korean War, Afghanistan, East Timor and Iraq.
Later marchers participated, earlier ones are descendants.
Enlisted men follow, then police, community groups and schools.
Scottish, brass and military bands drum the march.
Most of the town must be here.

A Kitty Hawk barrel rolls above High Street.
A youngish man sports a haircut and loose suit for the day
another looks like he walked off the farm.
Men show brief bonhomie; women are mostly silent;
children have distance in their eyes.
There seems a need for courtesy for silent sorrow.

Winter Shopping

The man pushing shopping trolleys outside
steams in his woollen hat and hi-vis jacket
while supermarket customers, comfortably sparse
joke and laugh with shop assistants.

An old man in a thick coat warms a bench
reading his newspaper near the frail Chinese lady
who sits straight-backed holding her walking stick upright.
Women smile through morning catch-ups.

At the coffee shop, two businessmen
talk earnestly; laptops on the table.
Continental banter fills the deli
as a toddler sprints over open tiles.

In offices near the mall
managers read numbers and worry
but here the morning smiles.

Finding the Calm Place

Taking the Break

The nervous respite lasts through mid-afternoon
while storm heads ride the wind from distant sea
to break the grip of this heat-record month.
Rain is drifting over the Brindabellas in hazes
between steaming hills and charcoal clouds.

Overhead the gloom is barely interrupted
as we grab the chance to trudge the hill.
Near the top a crimson rosella slouches
tail drooping, exhausted on the branch of a eucalypt.
An eastern grey kangaroo haunches, unwilling to move.

Down the breeze-cooled hillside currawongs are snapping;
a group harasses a peewee perched high;
nearby a pair chases a kestrel from above their claimed
feeding patch but lack the instant speed
to catch it before it glides to drop on unseen prey.

As we crunch back down, a wiry old man
grunts an unamused greeting through his teeth
then at the break near the crest half coughs half shouts
to claim yet another win from the hill.

Grand Affections

Grandfather worked with horse and sulky
as a country mailman in Bogabri.
Medical knowledge was lacking
so Nana watched her babies die;
eight out of eleven were lost
and most of her will with them.

Father's father was bombed and killed
at Tobruk a soldier for king and country
after lowering his age to re-enlist.
Dad was very fond of him.
Grandmother stayed at Concord in their home
where I lived with her while at uni.
She died of cancer when I was at sea.
I could not say goodbye.

As I navigated young life
I rarely thought about the love of grandparents.

Pushing Back

On the highway heavy trucks rumble
hauling their standard loads.
Sedans flash by barely laden;
tension begins to build
as cars around jostle.

This job is one I know
from before my eyes turned away.
The past returns
a little daunting – perhaps an adventure.
Business frontages are clean and crisp
on the road towards the desk.

Mixed-up Sunday

Saturday faces look dog-tired
like the working week is unended.
By midday Sunday that weariness has gone.
People are relaxed as they casually scan the shops
do their weekly shopping, buy a coffee or lunch
from cafes scented by the world's flavours.
Asian faces are here at Ryde; a few wear Muslim veils;
an African girl looks excited about the afternoon ahead;
old folks of Mediterranean extraction mix
with those of less obvious heritage
perhaps from England generations back.
No one seems to be concerned
unconsciously multicultural
while others elsewhere argue the issue.

On the hilltop the slim controller

stands supreme in grey-white.
Clusters of metal dishes talk and listen

from vantage points above the trees.
Barely noticed wires
own the near sky.

A line of silver posts hold
cameras to watch cars.
Digital prompts keep us at work.

The calling screens
steal hours from sleep
to build a second life

without human touch.
We formed them over decades
to serve us

but who obeys now?

In the Swim Again

I dunk my head for a second baptism
to retrieve the white quartz stone
the children have thrown for diving.

Looking up in bright dappled light
I see the agapanthus shine down
on what would have been my funeral time

but for the long avoided cut;
joining the shuffling queue
for chest spread to wrap a present

stitched to ache, twinge then calm.
This is second life. Are we sent
back like those from myth for iconic quests?

Yet for most our roles seem set;
no doubt new joys will emerge.

The Close Distance

In the red-brick church in Brunswick
the priest brings warm water to the font to baptise
the first child of a couple from the parish.
Family and friends smile – some are from interstate
one, like the father, from overseas.

For three years his mother had stitched
Carrickmacross lace in a Monaghan hamlet
to make a First Communion veil
for his sister. Now mother has sent it here
to grace the baptismal dress.

The baby with dark hair and connecting
smile, claimed her on a flying visit
before the icy northern winter.
The lace on-loan reminds of Grandma
and a vow to cherish.

Occasional Glow

The pensive man sitting nearby
tweed cap and neat shirt
on this Melbourne summer day
says he is two weeks from the big one.

The chemist's helper asks which birthday
so he answers eighty years.
She asks about his party plans.
Pausing he says he is in the slow lane

after fifty good years here.
He had come from snow-bound Durham
to do an air force job.
Later he brought back his wife

and stayed to raise a family.
Now he celebrates slowly.

Music of Belonging

Carriages jerk on the Flinders Street train.
Olive green silos for blue metal weather by tracks
to where the group sings and dances

with the youngest in the front;
women in national costume
with orange and lilac flowers embroidered;

golden cloth pinned with gold brooches.
Hair is drawn in buns
decorated with orchids or frangipani.

They sway to Peranakan songs
that thread through lives in the Straits;
and try to remember

murmurs of ancestors
on how to live the fruitful life.

Day Worker

Each day you take the road
looking for random work
this way, then another
stopping to work your art
on what is offered.

It isn't for the meagre money
that doesn't swell your store room.
You hope one day
what you make will bring a smile
and the need to visit again.

Closing the Circle

Barefoot paddocks of long grass with snakes, finches and skylarks
lured him from the child filled house and its stinging leather belt.
Ponds held tadpoles, small fish and leeches. Barbed wire and broken glass
carved slowly fading trophies. Abandoned market gardens gave crab apples
close to stands of eucalypts that stretched to the smelly mudflats
with crabs that scuttled into mangroves edging the coffee river

that flowed to the learning city built with broad-arrow sandstone
before brick canyons rose near the sea port to unsteady gate.
The harbour is curtained with cliffs that frame white caps of sea
near coasts where waves roar at trespassing land that stole her children aeons ago
even if they visit old mother in ships. A wallowing house with thick iron
walls and padded pipes was filled by drumming engines and the smell of diesel.

Outdoors he whistled to sunny porpoises that looked up, curious;
gulls, storm petrels and wandering albatross gleaned pickings from watery fields.
Waves and swell rose until they raged at stormy sky that stole the horizon
before the misty island of seals and penguins; north of cathedrals of ice;
a royal rookery teemed around rusted oil-rendering stills;
the windy plateau and gnarled basalts slowly retelling their story.

A flight away was the crowded lush land beneath heavy skies
   with its house near icy
pathways on Richmond Hill, and an elderberry bush that gave
   decent wine. Their first child
was born amid sleepless memory of frowns, and smiles of the
   West Indian midwife.
Railways stitch the city for pea-soup fogs and matchstick people
   walking doggedly
across Waterloo Bridge. There he firmed a profession to lead
   back to beginnings
to the leaf-green wooden house at the foot of Yellow Box Hill

where children grow and leave. Birds and kangaroos live in the
   woodland;
locals and wildlife see him on walks to ponder, visiting tree
   lined trails
completing his relearning with steadier tread.

www.ingramcontent.com/pod-product-compliance
Lightning Source LLC
Chambersburg PA
CBHW070936080526
44589CB00013B/1531